Songs for All Souls

Norbert Krapf

Fernwood
PRESS

Songs for All Souls

Fernwood Press
Newberg, Oregon
www.fernwoodpress.com

Printed in the United States of America

Cover and page design: Mareesa Fawver Moss

Cover art: Gregg Huebner

Cover photography: Tom Rockwell

Author photo: Andreas Riedel

ISBN 978-1-59498-117-3

for Katherine Trahan Krapf,
for persistently asking me
to collect these meditative poems

Contents

Acknowledgments

Some of these poems appeared in *Branches, Connotation Press: An Online Artifact, Tipton Poetry Journal,* and the anthologies *Rivers, Rails, and Runways* and *Airmail from the Airpoets,* (San Francisco Bay Press, 2008, 2011) by the Airpoets, Joyce Brinkman, Ruthelen Burns, Joseph Heithaus, Norbert Krapf, and Jeanie Dieter Smith. The translation of Rainer Maria Rilke's "Herbsttag/Fall Day" is from the author's *Shadows on the Sundial: Selected Early Poems* (Birmham Wood Graphics, 1990). Thanks to the editors, the late Elsa Kramer and Tom Healey, *Branches,* Kate Hillenbrand, *Connotation Press,* and Barry Harris of *The Tipton Poetry Journal* for giving some of these poems a home. And many thanks to Greg Heubner for his painting that is on the front cover and hangs in our house, as do other of his gorgeous paintings. Thanks also to Matthew Fox for his *Christian Mystics: 365 Readings and Meditations,* the inspiration for the poems in Section III, and to Wanda Wetli, model of listening and creator of spontaneous reflective prayer.

I believe that there is great wisdom in our species and Western spiritual traditions, but that this needs a new birth and a fresh beginning. As a Westerner I must begin where I stand within my own culture and its traditions.... We in the West must take these insights into our hearts on a regular basis, allow them to play in the heart, and then take them into our work and citizenship and family and community. This is how all healthy and deep awakenings happen; they begin with the heart and flow out from there.

—Matthew Fox, *Christian Mystics*

* * * * *

I wake to sleep and take my walking slow.
I feel my fate in what I cannot fear.
I learn by going where I have to go.

We think by feeling. What is there to know?
I hear my being dance from ear to ear.
I wake to sleep, and take my waking slow.

—Theodore Roethke, "The Waking"

I: All Souls Letter

All Souls Letter

Come back, all you spirits,
come back through the open
door & sit with us at the table.

Be kind & tell us what you learned.
Be patient & forgive us, if you can,
our daily ignorance & anxiety.

Help us see that not seeing
may be the best we can manage.
Give us hope that we can make

the long journey that you
took so well & arrive
in that realm where you live.

Help us believe that we
won't make a terrible mess
of this process of transformation

into a higher form of being.
Do not let us down as we pray
for guidance & good cheer.

Give us a seat in your boat.
Ferry us across the deep waters
toward that shore where light

opens & expands like a flower.
Come back, spirits, come back.
Lead us to the land where you live.

All Saints' Day, Erlangen, Germany

Whorls of gentian blue
beam bright between green

spikes & dark brown
linden leaves in the botanical

garden as the veil between
us & spirits stretches thin,

weather turns gray & raw,
& moisture assumes the shape

of snowflakes to descend
& ride on our shoulders.

Song for a Patron Saint

I go walking in the woods
& at every turn am met
by goblins, crooks, & creeps.
I turn & run away upset.

Patron saint, where are you
when I need you most?
Can't you help me
find the sacred host?

Down the empty streets
I look & search in vain
crying out like one left behind
running & reeling in the rain.

Patron saint, where are you
when I need you most?
Can't you help me
find the sacred host?

Anniversary

-for W.S. Merwin-

If every year we pass the day
on which the fire of our bodies
will stop burning, but spirit

will flame to another level,
& the silence of our griefs
& our joys will gather into

this higher burning, we must
prepare each day of every year
to become our future flame

so that those we leave
behind will hear our silence
& tune their ears to our

frequencies & see with
the help of the light we are
their world with new eyes.

In the Spirit House

Even when I was young I did
not think of cemeteries as sad.
To me they were quiet & peaceful
& housed spirits of those I loved.

When I became a father I often
brought my children to a cemetery
landscaped like a rural park.
We brought along a picnic lunch

& ate it & drank juice on a stone bench.
Sometimes we saw a rabbit or a pheasant
between tombstones. Periodically a diesel
commuter train ran along the back of the plot.

We played games & read books & I
pronounced the names carved in stone.
That world was populated with spirits
who became our friends, not enemies.

We did not walk in fear or dread.
We enjoyed the privacy of our park.
Nobody told us to go away.
Nobody told us to be quiet.

All That's Quiet

My friend is gone
who gave me light.

I look into the night
for anything bright

yearning to find
letters that form

to make lines in a song
someone will sing.

That song will name
what he was & did

& tell the story
of the love he left

for those who listen
to all that's quiet.

All the Singing

All the singing has subsided.
Late autumn: the gods decided
all sound must wind way down.
All the yearning birds have flown,
gone their migratory way.
Those that chose to stay
have nothing left to say.

From somewhere I hear
a faint song coming near,
of notes & words as dear
to me as the spirits of those
who faded like the rose
but stay with us here
in the turning of the year.

Passing Through

I pass through the hills
like a wind that blows
up & settles down.

You may hear me
rustle the leaves
on the banks of rivers.

Sometimes I drift
on the currents
& ride downstream.

Other times I meander
through valleys
& overflow in bottoms.

The red-tail hovers
above & looks down
on my invisible trail.

In the circle
of his watch
I am complete.

Sacred Places

(after photos by Denis Kelly)

1. Pilgrim Journey to Holy Lands

I fold my hands
near my heart,
close my eyes,
& wait for the light
to fill me with vision
so that my feet
can find their way
on the path that,
with help from beyond,
I pray to discover.

2. The Open Door

—Church of the Nativity,
Bethlehem—

After years of being
blinded by the light
I find & open
the door & step
inside radiant darkness.

Never have I seen
so well in the dark.
When my eyes close,
I see even better,
but when I leave

& re-enter the light,
I can see only the darkness
I carry with me from that
place inside where seeing
is not done by eye alone.

3. Desert Prayer

—desert monastery of St. George, near Jerusalem—

In the desert, morning sun
enters through our windows
& lifts us to prayer
that rises above shadow.

Afternoon sun coming
from the other direction
leaves us in shadows
that make us look within

for the light we
can summon only if
we give ourselves
to the kind of prayer that
transforms us into flame

as we feel desert heat
drop & descend to cold
that will settle in our hearts
unless the fire burns
within at the center.

4. Angel of Power and Protection

—Bridge to Vatican City, Rome—

What happens when the Angel
falls asleep after the mother
& father who held the baby
have to walk back into their lives

& the boy walks out into
the world & a servant
of God touches him wrong
when the parents aren't looking?

By the time he is ready to
cross the bridge to Vatican City
his feet will not move forward
but turn in the opposite direction

& it is decades before he
can talk to the old God
by finding his own sacred places
& a new language for praying.

5. Klara's Flame

—Klara Krapf, died Theresienstadt,
January 18, 1943—

You, flickering flame,
are the spirit of one
named Klara whose life
on earth came to
the wrong end

but who now
lives in memory
we consecrate by
saying & repeating
your name so that

the flame you
have become is fanned
by our breath when we say:
We remember Klara Krapf.
We commemorate Klara.

6. Memory Composed Out of Dust

—St. Paul's Chapel, Ground Zero—

Days after flame ignited
all into dust & ash
I step out onto the front porch
twenty-four miles to the east
on an Island that is Long,
to find out what is that smell.

I inhale invisible particles of dust
that are residue of buildings
& human flesh & bone
& now the remains of spirit
that become part of me
which I carry inland
three years later
when I move to Indiana.

Six years beyond the return
west I compose this prayer
out of their spirit to remember
those who breathed with us.

II: Morning Meditations

Matins

Sing, sweet soul,
your essential song;
eye on the goal,
the journey long.

Morning Prayer

Open these eyes
& this spirit
to the world
I love

so the pen
I hold finds
the right words
to give praise

to what
I will leave
behind.

Morning Devotions

My mother is picking tomatoes
in the warm morning sun

wearing a blue apron,
her kitchen uniform.

One tomato in her palm
is the blessing she gives.

Behind her, in memory,
her mother & grandmother.

They all genuflect cupping
a round red chalice in hand.

Language of Leaves

How many trees
can we name
from their leaves?

If we cannot name
what is beneath our feet,
how well do we walk?

When my father
taught me to name trees,
what power did he give?

Without naming,
what language
would we speak?

Without a language,
what world
could we bless?

Deep in Woods

In the woods
early morning
sounds begin.

To listen
is to be
open wide.

What we hear
is who we
become.

If we hear
what is
not there

we are
somewhere
else.

The more
we open

the deeper
we stand.

Six Morning Meditations

1. Query

If the firefly is only
an insect in daylight,
do I glow in the dark?

2. Spring Rite

White pear blossoms drift
onto the floor of the open café
where we savor silence.

3. Dogwood

Below the window sill
beside my wife's maple desk,
dogwood buds open in light.

4. Honey Locust

Tiny green leaves opening
on the branch almost touch
our black balcony rail.

5. Crocus Petals

Flakes of color
ready to sleep
forever in the soil.

6. Interior Blossom

Wind whistles around
my corner windows.
Poems blossom inside.

An Octave a Day

Love shines
like the sun
on us below.

This heaviness
I carry lifts
note by note.

Each note we
play builds
a scale of grace.

Climb an octave a day
& this weight
may go away.

Downtown

Wherever we go,
the green life
comes along.

Brought lilies from
that island world:
they, too, revived.

When irises open,
we come every morning
to worship in silence.

German sage drinks
up rain water at the base
of the downspout.

Beside electric box:
pink & white petals
of flowering almond

from the garden of
my great-grandparents
in the hill country.

Cultivating

The flowers bloom
whether we are
rich or poor.

Without the blue
of the iris, where
would heaven be?

When my mother
watered her flower beds,
she hummed as she poured.

Her flowers
open every year
in my mind.

City Sounds

Throughout the night,
call & response
of freight trains.

Wake up to doves
love-cooing from
the roof gutters.

Music finds
& uplifts me
wherever I go.

Walt Whitman
caught the pitch
of street song.

Hum of tire on
pavement, fading
wail of siren.

Wind whistles high
around the corners
of the townhouse.

Minor Key

Red-tailed hawk
you lift me
into your vortex.

Snow-white hepatica
you keep my eyes
on the ground.

Bottom-loving carp
you pull me
to the depths.

Dove in the pine
I coo in
your minor key.

Fallen Feather

Dove flutters
down onto
balcony rail.

She eyes
flower box
for nest.

She sees
me looking
staring at her.

Dove pulls up
& away:
feather falls.

Feather settles
beside the green
of chives.

Dove's dark
eye floats
in memory.

III: The Smallest Sprout

Divinity Sings

Sometimes I hear Divinity sing
at night or during the day.
Sometimes she sings quietly,
sometimes he sings vigorously.
Every time I hear this music
I rise a little higher
in my seat,
my eyes see farther,
and my ears open wider.

Sunday Morning Prayer

Let the day
join hands with the night.
Let the left
& right brains
work together
& may the night
give off light.

Religious Wars

O religious wars
in which we give
ourselves license
and a blessing
to murder one another!

Division

There is a prayer
in every atom
waiting to divide
into more prayer
ad aeternam
amen.

Tuning

The more in tune
we are with
the universe

the better we sing
the psalms
we compose.

Deepest Rhythm

Our deepest rhythm
is in the pulse
that binds us
to all that lives
and breathes as one.

Prepared Heart

The heart prepared to die
knows how to come
back & beat slow
with the joy
of life affirmed.

Awakened Eyes

Listening & looking
into the eyes
of the awakened
we see & follow
a flame that shows
us the way.

Stone Mute

Oh to be stone mute
& let the vibrations
come through us
& wake us
to a mouth
through which
we make sound.

Smallest Sprout

The smallest sprout
is the biggest miracle.

Earthy Goddess

Oh earthy goddess,
lie down in my bed
& awaken me
to the depths
of my soul.

Homecoming

I come home
to the spirit
in my flesh
& am attached
to atoms whirling
within & around
where I walk.

Nothing

I am nothing
full of everything.

Rebirth

I die into myself
& am reborn
in you.

Spirit Song

Prayer comes
from the eye
that beholds,
the voice
that would sing,
the spirit
that can no longer
rest in silence.

Wordless

When I look at you
I pray deeply
though no words
come from my mouth.

Garden Liturgy

Pulling weeds
deadheading flowers
pouring water
are my liturgy.

Runes

I find a rune
in the grace
of the air

& sing a song
of what I see
everywhere.

Cloth

If we are interwoven
we are of one cloth.

Completion

I am blessed
to be incomplete
because I complete myself
by merging with others.

Creation

**When I create anything
I participate in
all creation.**

Gods & Religions

When we worship
the sacred around us
all gods & religions
celebrate their liturgy.

IV. After Waking in the Dark

Woods Song

When I was a boy
I was happiest
in the woods

where I watched
light filter down
through the trees

& heard the songs
of birds & insects
in just the right pitch.

I knew then
I could never find
a better way to pray

than to receive
this combination
of sight & song.

Saying the Name

As a rule it is better for a man
to name God in his native tongue
than in one that is foreign to him.
　　　　　—Simone Weil

I would say your name
in my native tongue
so that you rise
from within me
& the history
of my people
& the language
we speak & the spirit
of this place
that is home to us
& nourishes us
with its fruits
& is part
of your great spirit
that gives us love
of ourselves & one
another & all spirit.

Vision Song

Spirit so beautiful
come down to us
as mother of all
and touch us
in song & let us
breathe in your essence
& lift us up
body & soul
& take us where
we long to go
& live & bless us
with vision that
opens all eyes
& brings us
together so we
are one & sing
our small parts
in the chorus
of voices that
gives glad praise
to the beauty
of the spirit
thrumming through
the creation
you consecrate
& give to us.

Born into the Beyond

for Marilyn, stillborn sister

Baby girl, little sister
born into the beyond
you are the wind in my hair,
the sun on my skin.

Baby girl, little sister
born into the beyond
you are the song in my heart,
the poem in my fingertips.

Baby girl, little sister
born into the beyond
you are the breath in my mouth,
the blood in my veins.

Baby girl, little sister
though born into the beyond
you appear in the present
& call me to a life to come.

Seeing the Light

—for Helen, Michael, and Dominic—

I saw the light at the end
of a candle enter into the eyes

of a baby over whose forehead
a priest poured baptismal water.

As the baby's eyes reflected back
the light which beamed onto the faces

of his parents, I prayed for grace
to enter into our hearts as light came

into his eyes so that we can all live
with the love & compassion

that will make us unite
as we see the light

that transforms us into a nation
of many finally become one.

Credo

My allegiance is to what
grows in out-of-the-way places,

people who return to
where they come from,

song that arises from
and celebrates the place

that gave birth to it,
& spirit that

derives its strength
from a source

deep in the earth
that constantly renews

itself even though
few know its name

or give it credit
for its potency.

Father Loss

I remember how glad we all were
to be together again, despite the sorrow,
& expressed our relief too vigorously.

So I shushed everyone, as if someone
must take charge, & as the eldest,
hugged our mother, who was sobbing

with a grief thousands of years old.
She was wracked by the sudden
loss of the man who fathered us,

her children, who was her mate
& companion for decades.
I neither had nor needed words.

Our bodies clung together
as only survivors can. Her
grief grabbed hold of me

& carried me with her shaking
as we rode together the bucking
waves of the waters of loss.

Meditation on Yearning

We live by the ancient rhythms,
of the seasons within the cycles
of life & death while

trying to discover meaning in
the particulars of our existence,
but if we descend too deeply

into the particular & never
move beyond the national
or remain trapped in the local

we suffer an inability to
connect with & ride those
ancient rhythms & so we

yearn to live within the particular
so fully that we are released
into the universal, live in time

but move beyond it, love
fervently where we are but yearn
finally for what lies beyond.

After Waking in the Dark

I want to break wide open
under the dark night sky
beneath the trees that
are shedding their leaves
& as those leaves
drift toward the earth
I want to become wings
that lift upward until
they catch a rhythm
that is ecstacy incarnate
& stand outside myself
like spirit soaring
into the highest reaches
of being it can become
as the night sky
opens into blue day
I recognize as home.

Small Love Song

Let us live as if no line
between here & there
can come between us.

One Ounce

Give me one ounce
of insight in a sea
of uncertainty

& I'll bob to
the surface
of the water

I thought would
pull me under
& take me down.

Direct

I am lucidity
gliding toward you,
refusing to hide

in the fake
complexity
of academia.

I come at you
with all I am, trans-
parent as sunlight.

Longing for Blue

How we all live
& long for blue,
of the sky when
clouds hang over,

for the water
when it opens
into an expanse
of salty sea,

for the color
of an eye
when a lid lifts
& invites us in,

but how little
we want our mood
to sink & settle

into what we turn
plural as a state
we call "the blues."

Moon Float

I would bathe
in her nimbus

& then let go
& float in whatever

direction her tides
take me, open to

whatever influence
she wishes to exert,

whatever pull she
may have that leaves

me stranded on any
new shore, rising

to enter into the next
phase ready to wax.

Shift in Belief

Even when our burden
appears to lie heaviest
upon us, its dominion
every day decreases
by a few moments.

Each day we breathe
a little more easily,
even if we cannot see
our daily dose of more
relief that brings us closer
to the moment when

we can feel that shift
that means we have
come through once again

& earned the right
to believe in rebirth.

As the Earth

I would be as the earth
that lies waiting to receive
the hoof print of the deer.

I would wear your print
as a lover who tingles
when warm lips touch his.

However your feet touch
upon me would give me
the satisfaction of bearing
witness to the miracle
of your being.

Step gently.

Feel me breathe
beneath you
with the spirit
of the leavings
of all who live
& die here.

When the Sensual

When the sensual
lies down with the spiritual

the right flowers open
in light, first the irises

& then the lilies followed
by the evening primroses,

& the right birds
sing in the branches

that look down upon
all the blossoming,

the robins in the honey locust,
the cardinals in the dogwood,

& the sun shines warm
from a rising perspective.

And when the daylight sinks
down into the delicious dark

the sensual folds once
again into the spiritual

& the constellations
bloom white above.

Short Shadows

I stood often
in the shadows
of a short father
& uncles

but knew even
then that the length
of a man's shadow
was no measure

of his will,
his spirit,
or the depth
of his love

They Always Knew

Always behind the men
who spoke the word
were the women who
quietly made the house

& kept the family
together & knew
what to do when
a child came sobbing

& what to say
when the world went
wrong & how
to hug when no

doctor could be
found or the priest
had no time to
give his blessing.

Hey, Little Circe

Hey, little Circe, little Siren,
how come you sing in my ear?

You think you know something I don't?
How come you lean into me

& breathe so warm on my lips?
How you know so well where to move?

Can't you see the whole picture?
Don't you remember where I go

after your spell dwindles to gone?
Back to my muse, the one who

stays with me for the course,
knows how to endear & endure.

So Many Mornings

So many mornings
the first light
finds me sitting
at my desk

ready to move forward
into one of the remaining
days of my life
eager to discover

whatever it may bring
that I have never experienced,
something that I may come
to understand more fully,

see a leaf fall
at a different angle,
hear a great song sung
in a new way,

a familiar voice
speak to me
with a kind of love
I had not detected.

Levels

The root
of our being
bores down

deeper to
find & tap
the deepest water

to make our
green parts
grow stronger

in the light
of the sun
burning above.

The Sycamore & the River

The sycamore stays home
beside its familiar river,
has no inclination to roam.

It has faith in its roots
to draw the water
that makes it grow strong.

But for us it's not wrong,
in search of our home,
to wander & roam

far and wide & long
& then put down roots
to tap the deepest waters

that help us feel at home,
convince us we belong,
keep our spirit strong.

Fall Day

(after Rainer Maria Rilke)

Lord, the time's come. The summer's full.
Lay your shadows on the sundials,
set the winds free across the fields.

Make the last fruits full;
give them two more southerly days,
push them to completion and drive
the last sweetness into full-bodied wine.

Whoever has no house now won't build one.
Whoever is alone will be alone a long time,
will stay awake, read, write long letters,
and will wander restlessly here and there
along the avenues when the leaves blow.

Spirits Floating

(after the paintings of Greg Huebner)

Spirits float through the universe
in different shapes & sizes
of colors & combinations

& I am one myself & like
to look at & admire the colors
others bring into my life & think

about how they became who
& what they are & where
they may be going & see if

perhaps we are alike & come
together to form new constellations
of color & shape & patterns

of a particular inclination
or possible combinations
of clusters that form

new arrangements of planets
that float together in different
but somehow related fields

of lights & darks & bursts
of spiritual intensities & songs
that only some can perceive

& sing & appreciate as we
beam toward one another lending
our little lights to the galaxies

of longings & light years
of rays & capabilities of brilliance
we all contribute to one another.

Author Biography

Norbert Krapf, former Indiana Poet Laureate, a native of Jasper, Indiana, is the author of fifteen poetry collections, including the recent *Indiana Hill Country Poems, Southwest by Midwest, Spirit Sister Dance,* and *Catholic Boy Blues.* He is the author of the memoirs *The Ripest Moments: A Southern Indiana Childhood, Shrinking the Monster: Healing the Wounds of Our Abuse,* and the recent *Homecomings: A Writer's Memoir,* which covers the fifty years of his writing and publishing life. He is the winner of the Lucille Medwick Memorial Award from the Poetry Society of America, A Glick Indiana Author Award, and a Creative Writing Fellowship from the Arts Council of Indianapolis, for combining poetry and the blues.

He has released a poetry and jazz CD, *Imagine,* with pianist-composer Monika Herzig and performs poetry and the blues with Gordon Bonham. He has a poem in stained glass at the Indianapolis International Airport, and his poems have been read on the Writer's Almanac. He has also translated *Shadows on the Sundial: Selected Early Poems of Rainer Maria,* a collection of legends from his ancestral Franconia, *Beneath the Cherry Sapling,* and edited and annotated pioneer German journals, letters, and other documents from his native Dubois County, Indiana, in *Finding the Grain.*

Title Index

First Line Index

Printed in the USA
CPSIA information can be obtained
at www.ICGtesting.com
CBHW011117020324
4861CB00006B/80

9 781594 981173